# Benny Goes to Bed by Himself

**Kids and parents**
Beating Nighttime Fears Together

**Dr. Jonathan Kushnir**
Ram Kushnir

# Benny Goes to Bed by Himself

By: Dr. Jonathan Kushnir, Ram Kushnir

Printed in the United States of America

First Printing, 2020

ISBN 9798636025238

Please visit us online for more information.
Our web page: www.bennygoes2bed.com
Facebook: www.facebook.com/NighttimeFears/

# Introduction for the reading parent:

The process of going to bed and falling asleep can be a serious and stressful challenge, especially for young children. Many children experience the night and the "getting to sleep" moments as an anxious process, in a way that makes them feel distressed, which affects the entire family.

This book is intended to help parents and children overcome fear and overcome it calmly and consciously. The story incorporates the principles of cognitive-behavioral therapy for dealing with difficulties—and offers a light and clear way of coping. The book describes a kind of roadmap that helps build a pathway that will help the child and his or her parents move in the direction of solving the problem.

In addition, throughout the book are explanations for parents, which describe the therapeutic principles utilized in the story and offer knowledge to help the process.

Also, behind the illustrations, you will find a whole world, subject to a common interpretation: child and parent.

*Please note that this book is not a substitute for treatment by a qualified professional.*

Once upon a time, there was a lion cub.
A cute little lion cub named **Benny**.

Benny lived in **Africa** with Mom and Dad
in a place where the sun shines bright and
warm, under the broad and green trees that
were his home.

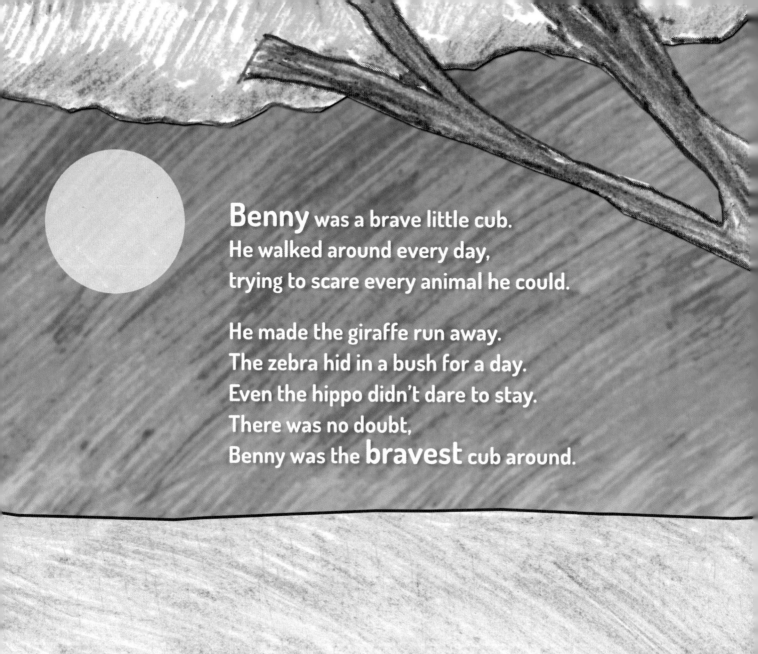

**Benny** was a brave little cub.
He walked around every day,
trying to scare every animal he could.

He made the giraffe run away.
The zebra hid in a bush for a day.
Even the hippo didn't dare to stay.
There was no doubt,
Benny was the **bravest** cub around.

But at night, Benny was a little less brave.
Every time he went to bed,
**scary thoughts** would fill his head.

What kind of **thoughts,** you ask?
The strangest you can think of.

**Scary beasts** that are hairy and mean,
and creatures of shapes like you've never seen.

Benny would lie in bed and stare into the night,
and though nothing was there,
his imagination went wild.

"Ugh. . .it's too warm and I'm covered in sweat,
I think a scary creature is getting
close to my bed," he would think to himself as
he tossed and turned, with quick, shallow breaths
and a pounding heart.

**For the parents:**
As part of the normal physiological response to a threatening situation and the
preparation to deal with it, a variety of sensations may be felt. For example, accelerated
pulse, sweating, rapid breathing. These sensations typically diminish and disappear
as the sense of threat passes.

A lot of times, Benny would try to clear
his head of **scary thoughts.**

He would **imagine** good things,
like cute furry creatures, candy, presents,
and **warm hugs** from Mom and Dad.

But each and every time, the opposite occurred:
bad thoughts would return to Benny's head,
**scaring** the good thoughts away.

The presents were gone, the candy turned sour,
and the cute creatures fled at full power.

**For the parents:**
Sometimes, in order to deal with fears, we try to drive away scary or unpleasant thoughts
by creating a distraction or by thinking about something else. Usually, as a result of
this action, the scary thoughts soon return. Try not to think of a pink rabbit for the next
two minutes and raise your hand whenever it bounces back into your head.

Ask yourself, "How many times have I raised my hand?"

And so, every night, Benny was alone
with his scary thoughts.

"I can't take it!" he thought to himself.

"I'm scared. The creatures are frightening and big,
and I'm just a little cub!"

And how could Benny sleep through such distress?
Only one thing could put an end to this mess.

"Mommy! Daddy!" Benny would shout as loud as
he could, waking all other cubs sleeping in the neighborhood.

**For the parents:**
Most often, because of a desire for the child to go to sleep quickly, or as a result of helplessness
facing the child's situation, parents either stay close to the child, or the child sleeps in the parents'
bed as a way to deal with his/her night fears.

However, despite the fact that this approach may work in the short term, in the long run, this does
not allow the child to learn that he or she is capable of dealing with their fears. Moreover, it creates
a dependency on the parent. As a result, the child won't be able to learn that even if the parent is not
there, the scary thing will not actually occur. In addition, the child learns that the scary sensations
"require" the parent's involvement. Finally, children who depend on their parents to go to sleep will
extend their sleeping time and increase the number of nighttime wake-ups.

Mom or Dad always came, yawned, and sat next to Benny.
"It's those creatures again. The **strange sounds** and scary
shadows. . ." Benny would say.

Mom and Dad, who themselves were really tired,
would stay quietly beside his bed, caressing his little head,
and **wait patiently** until he was asleep.

Benny's mom and dad would sometimes
get a little angry and say,

"**Stop!** When are you going to go to sleep
 by yourself? You are supposed to be **a brave lion!**"

Benny would quietly reply, "I know. I'm sorry.
I honestly didn't want to **disturb** you;

but I've got to have someone **on guard**,
making sure there are no monsters around."

**For the parents:**

Parents often express anger out of frustration and present unreasonable demands to the child. Doing so leads to a worsening situation. This will make it more difficult for the child to cope with his or her fears and, in turn, make it more difficult for them to successfully go to sleep.

The correct response is to validate the child's fears: "I know it's hard for you, but. . ." and aim to carry out a structured and gradual program of how to properly cope with the fear.

Benny continued to **wake up** Mom and Dad every night.

Everyone was **tired**.

Mom was **yawning**. Dad almost fell asleep in the middle of supper, and only Benny slept late, because he was a lion cub and he didn't have to get up early for work.

When he finally got up, he would think to himself how much he'd like to be able to **go to sleep** without anyone's help.

One morning (after a long night during which Benny woke up Mom and Dad at least twice!), the lion family strolled to the lake for water.

On the way to the lake, they saw Alfred.
Alfred was an old and very wise lion.

"Oh, we're so glad to see you!"
Benny's dad said to Alfred.

"Perhaps you can give us some advice?"
Alfred replied, "I'll help anyone, of course, whether it's a lion, zebra, or horse!"

Dad explained, "We'd really like to **help** our cute cub
Benny learn how to **go to bed by himself**.

He tries really hard, but he can't.
What do you think we can do?"

21

Alfred turned to Benny and asked,
"Can you tell me what's **bothering** you at night?"

"When I go to sleep, I **imagine** all sorts of evil
and scary things," said Benny.

"And these scary things, do they **really exist?**"
Alfred asked.

"I know they don't really exist,
but at night, after the sun disappears,
they **feel real**, as if something is actually near!"

**For the parents:**

The reaction to fear, both physical and behavioral, will occur not only in a "truly dangerous" situation but also in a situation where there's a perception or belief that the situation is dangerous.

Young children who suffer from fear find it difficult to distinguish between the real and the imaginary. This can increase their fears.

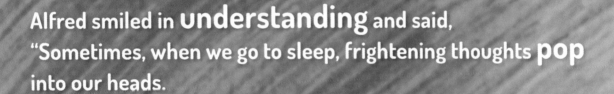

Alfred smiled in **understanding** and said,
"Sometimes, when we go to sleep, frightening thoughts **pop**
into our heads.

Thoughts that are strange and phony.
It's as if someone's sitting in there, making up scary stories."
"How do we make this phony–someone **go away?**"
Benny asked.

"First, **naming** this villain would be a great assistance," Alfred replied while stroking his whiskers.
"What name would you like to give it?
"Can I pick any name I want?" Benny asked.
"Of course."

Benny thought for a minute and said,
"I'll call him 'Tricksy'!"

"That's a great name!" said Alfred.
"From now on, when bad thoughts appear at night, remember that it's just Tricksy playing tricks in your head, making up scary stories when you lie in your bed."

**For the parents:**

One of the methods that can help a child is "externalization"—that is, to distinguish between the scary thoughts the child has and reality. Giving a name to the scary process will help the child treat fear as something that can and must be dealt with. You can give all kinds of names to fear, for example, The Bully, The Monster, Grumpy, Goofy, Tricksy, etc.

Alfred continued, "And to get rid of Tricksy,
you have to learn to go to sleep without Mom and Dad.
I know it sounds very hard indeed.

But following the right path,
every lion can **succeed**. Look over there,"
Alfred said and pointed to a group of trees.

In one of the trees sat a baby monkey
who wanted to jump from a low branch onto
a higher one. It seemed that the little monkey
was afraid he wouldn't make it.

For a few seconds, the **monkey** sat and **thought**.
Suddenly, he jumped and grabbed another branch—a closer one.

From there, he grabbed a branch that was a little higher, and
then another one, and only then did the little monkey
 reach the **highest** branch.

28

"I've got it!" Benny said.
"The monkey moved from one branch to the other,
**one step at a time**,
until he reached the top branch **safe** and sound;
instead of jumping high and falling to the ground."

Alfred smiled and said, "My **clever** cub, that is correct.
And like the monkey, we'll fight your **fear** step by step.

Mom and Dad will stay with you less and less each night
that passes, until you can go to sleep **by yourself**."

The lion family said **goodbye** to Alfred.
They were so happy they had a plan.

"If we make an **effort** and work together,
we will get rid of Tricksy forever!"

Benny said to himself hopefully,
waiting for night to come.

Night fell and it was time to go to bed.
Benny's mom caressed his head and said,
**"Good night**, sweet son.

If you look over your shoulder.
I'll be over there, on that boulder."
She pointed to a large rock that was not far
from Benny's bed.

Benny was a little **worried** when he heard Mom's
footsteps moving away. But still, he felt ready for the
**challenge** and closed his eyes.

**For the parents:**

Like any coping process, overcoming fear has to be done gradually, in small doses—ones that the child is capable of dealing with, despite being afraid. Slowly and gradually, after a certain degree of security has been achieved, the level of difficulty can be increased. Persistence is required here.

You can also come up with levels with the child and at each level, indicate the next "task." After every success, you can mark the "task" as completed in any creative way you see fit.

It was **dark** and quiet.
After a short while, **frightening thoughts**
started crawling into Benny's head.
He imagined scary things approaching.
"**Tricksy** is making up scary stories again," he thought.

Benny tried to **fight** his fears and ignore the bad
thoughts, until he felt it was too hard for him.

When Benny woke up, this time early in the morning,
he was **thrilled** he'd made it without calling his parents.
**Mom and Dad** were **very happy** as well.

"You started great; really well done!
We are so proud of our son!
But remember, our work has just **begun.**"

The following night, before bedtime, Mom told Benny that tonight, she'd sit a little further away: under the tree next to the big rock. Benny **nodded** and closed his eyes.

After a short while, as usual, he started to imagine scary things. "It's **Tricksy again** trying to scare me," he thought to himself.

Benny tried to clear his head of those thoughts. Suddenly there was a windy whistle: "**Whooosshhhhh.**"

Benny panicked. "Oh no! What was that?! Something bad is getting close. I think I smell it with my nose!" he fearfully thought to himself and felt his heart pounding.
Benny opened his eyes and looked around: "**Where's Mom?**" he thought.

Benny's mother came and gave him a hug.
"I heard a loud howling bark,
and thought that someone was hiding in the dark,"
Benny said in a trembling voice.

"Remember, my dear, it's only Tricksy trying to scare you.
Now we need to be **strong**, do our best, and carry on."
Mom stepped away back to the tree.
Benny calmed down, closed his eyes, and fell asleep.

In the morning, Benny woke up and thought of last night.
He was concerned. **Beating Tricksy** suddenly
seemed like the hardest challenge he'd ever faced. . .

But Benny decided not to let go.
"If I stay strong without giving up,
Tricksy's nonsense will finally stop,"
he said to himself with **confidence.**

**For the parents:**
Children use self-talk to help themselves cope with fear.
For example, "I won't let fear beat me. It's scary at first, but if I don't give
up, my fears will decrease."

42

Benny **did not give up.**
The following nights, Mom and Dad sat farther and
farther away, until one night, when Benny went
to bed, his father said, "It will be a little harder
tonight. I will sit totally out of your sight."
"Totally out of sight?!" Benny was worried.

"Yes, but I'll come to visit every few minutes
until you're asleep, and you'll keep on
**doing great** as you have so far."

Dad gave Benny a lion's goodnight kiss,
and walked away from his bed until he was gone.

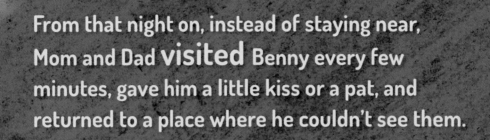

From that night on, instead of staying near, Mom and Dad **visited** Benny every few minutes, gave him a little kiss or a pat, and returned to a place where he couldn't see them.

They came back again and again until Benny was asleep.

**For the parents:**

There's great importance in executing the program consistently. Additionally, when the parent "visits" the child, he or she must stay with the child only for a few seconds. Either fix the blanket, send a kiss in the air, or just have the child see you, then get out of the room. It is important to avoid getting into a discussion or conversation surrounding the child's fears.

Although there is reassurance in the parent's presence, in order for the child to be able to cope with his or her fears without the parent, it is better to direct him or her to handle his or her fears alone.

Every passing night,
Benny stayed alone in bed for a longer time.
He was pretty **surprised**, that even when
Mom and Dad were nowhere near,
no evil creature actually appeared.

And so, Benny's nights passed with short visits.
There were nights when he fell asleep **without any help!**
On others, when his fears suddenly arose,
he didn't let Tricksy disturb his pleasant doze.

One morning, Benny woke up,
went to Mom and Dad and said,

**"I can go to sleep by myself!**

I feel I can overcome Tricksy on my own!"
Benny's parents were **so proud.**

"What an absolute delight.
From now on, we can sleep a full night,"
they said and hugged Benny, their **brave cub.**

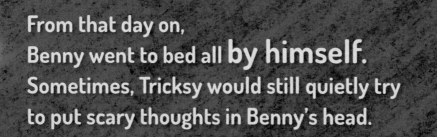

From that day on,
Benny went to bed all **by himself.**
Sometimes, Tricksy would still quietly try
to put scary thoughts in Benny's head.

But Benny knew he shouldn't be scared,
because the strange faces and scary beasts
were **imaginary** things that **did not exist!**

He would close his eyes and fall asleep with ease.
His parents were also sleeping peacefully,
enjoying the African breeze.

**For the parents:**
Through the gradual process, Benny developed a self-soothing ability, which helped him overcome his fears, and as a result, he was able to go to sleep independently.
Over time, he began sleeping alone, without waking up continuously every night.

Now that Benny knows how to
go to sleep **on his own,**
he walks around Africa, teaching other
cubs how to get rid of the Tricksies
in their heads, and how to sleep
**without fear** all by themselves.

# Dr. Kushnir

## Clinical Psychologist

Dr. Jonathan Kushnir is a clinical psychologist, an expert and an instructor in Cognitive Behavior Therapy, accredited by the European Association for Behavioral Therapies.

After completing his Ph.D. in clinical psychology in Israel and a research fellowship in the U.S, he has successfully treated for over a decade thousands of children and adults suffering from anxieties and sleep disorders. His insightful articles on the subject have been published in top scientific - peer reviewed journals.

"The idea for this book was born after treating numerous children and their parents and observing their rough and frustrating struggles with nighttime fears and accompanying sleep difficulties.
In this book we aim to deliver the knowledge accumulated over the years in a simple and unique way; one that can be easily understood by kids and adults alike.

**We hope this book will guide you successfully on your road to overcome this stubborn problem."**

If you enjoyed my book, it would be great if you left a review to let others know that they, too, can benefit from this book.

Your review will also help me see what is and isn't working so I can better serve all my readers.

**Scan to add a review:**